If You Give a Bear a Bong

PRINCE

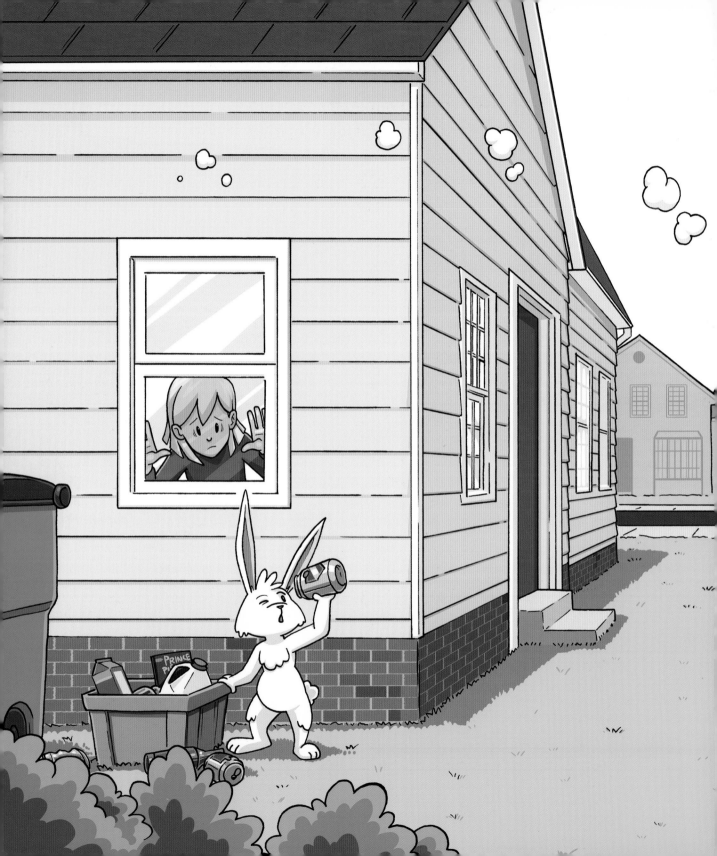

If You Give a Bear a Bong

Written by **Sam Miserendino**

Illustrated by **Mike Odum**

Skyhorse Publishing

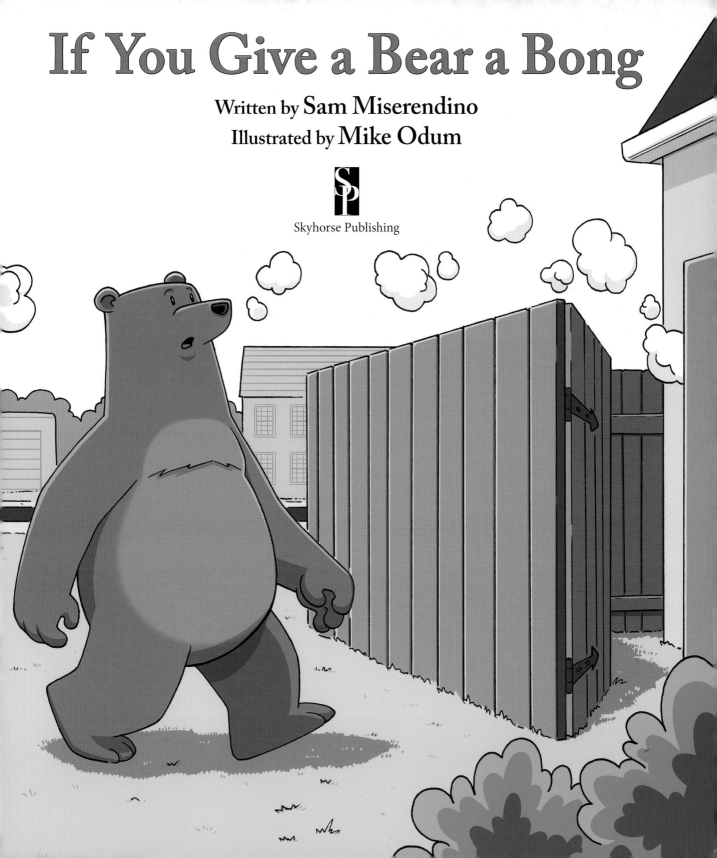

Skyhorse Publishing books may be purchased in bulk at special discounts for sales promotion, corporate gifts, fund-raising, or educational purposes. Special editions can also be created to specifications. For details, contact the Special Sales Department, Skyhorse Publishing, 307 West 36th Street, 11th Floor, New York, NY 10018 or info@skyhorsepublishing.com.

Skyhorse® and Skyhorse Publishing® are registered trademarks of Skyhorse Publishing, Inc.®, a Delaware corporation.

Visit our website at
www.skyhorsepublishing.com.

10 9 8 7 6 5 4 3 2 1

Library of Congress Cataloging-in-Publication Data is available on file

Cover and interior artwork by Mike Odom

Print ISBN: 978-1-5107-3396-1

E-Book ISBN: 978-1-5107-3402-9

Printed in China

Special Thanks To:
Tosca Miserendino
Stacie Odum
Jack W. Perry
Don Loudon
Ron Riffle
Jeanne Miserendino
Beverly Miserendino
Travis Bundy
Shawn Gates

BLIMPSHARKZ

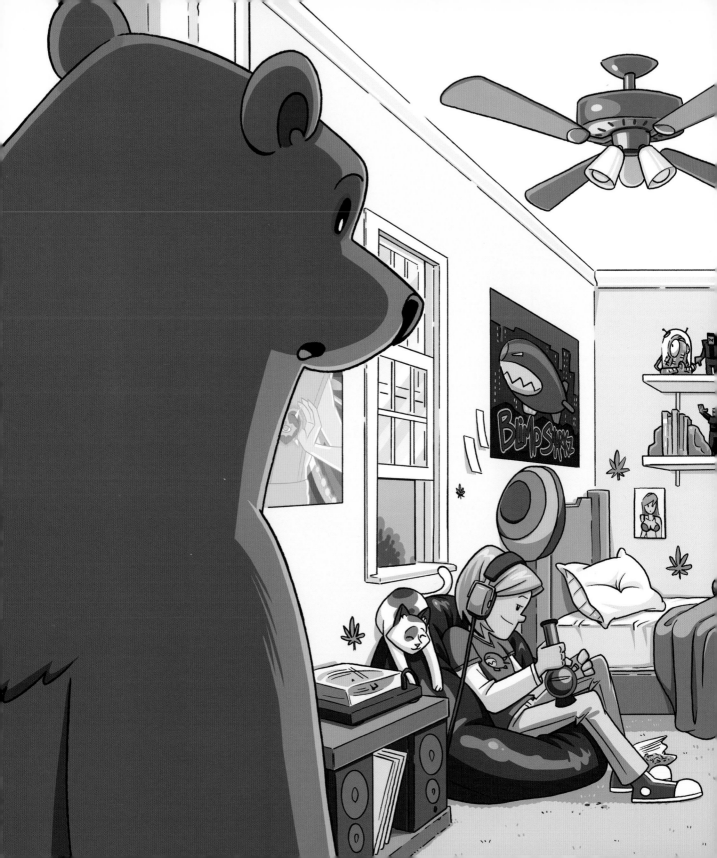

If you give a bear a bong,

he'll ask if you're a cop.

When you tell him
that you're not,

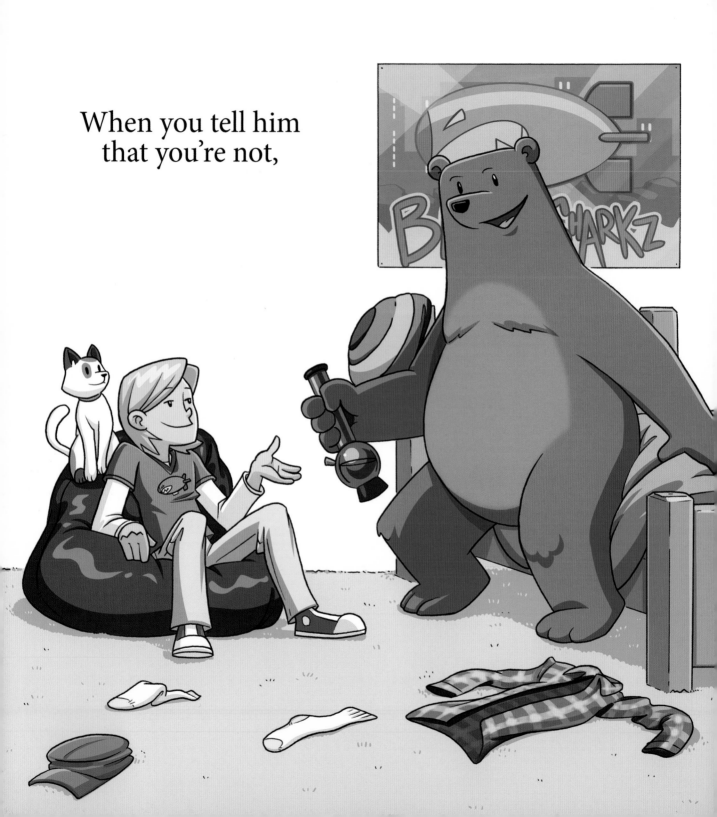

he'll take one hit…

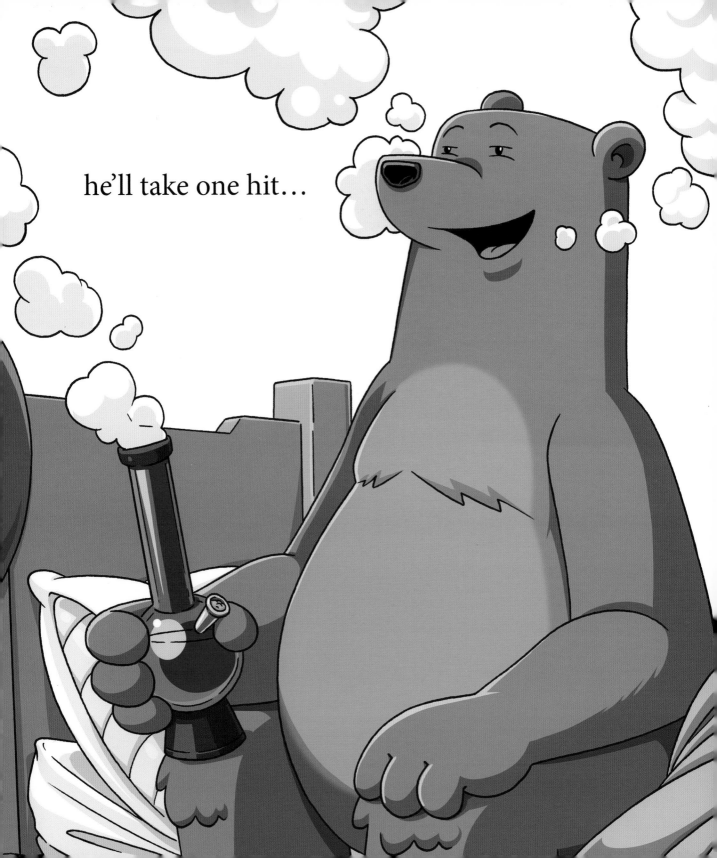

Then another...

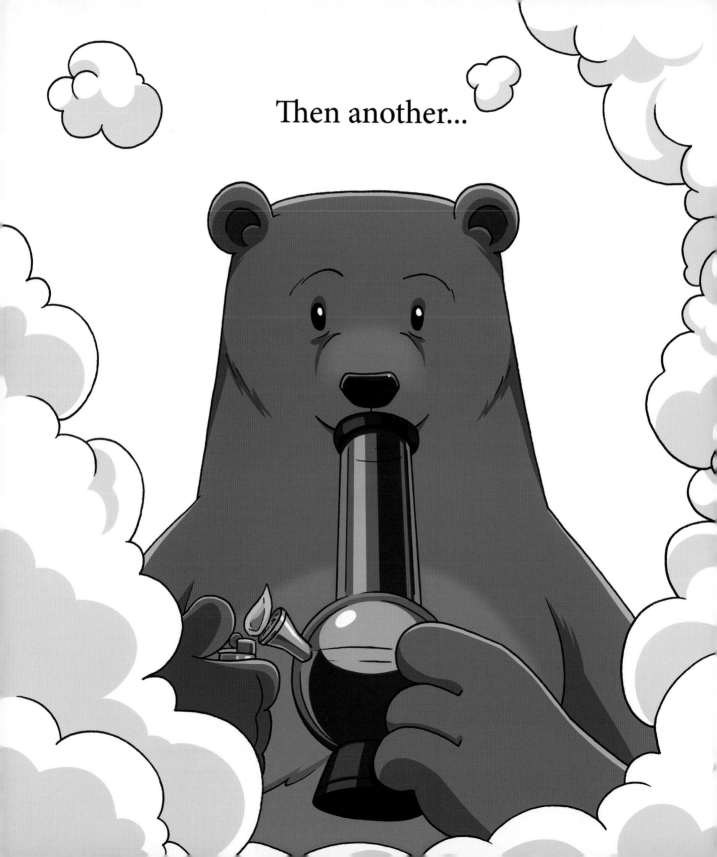

And
another...

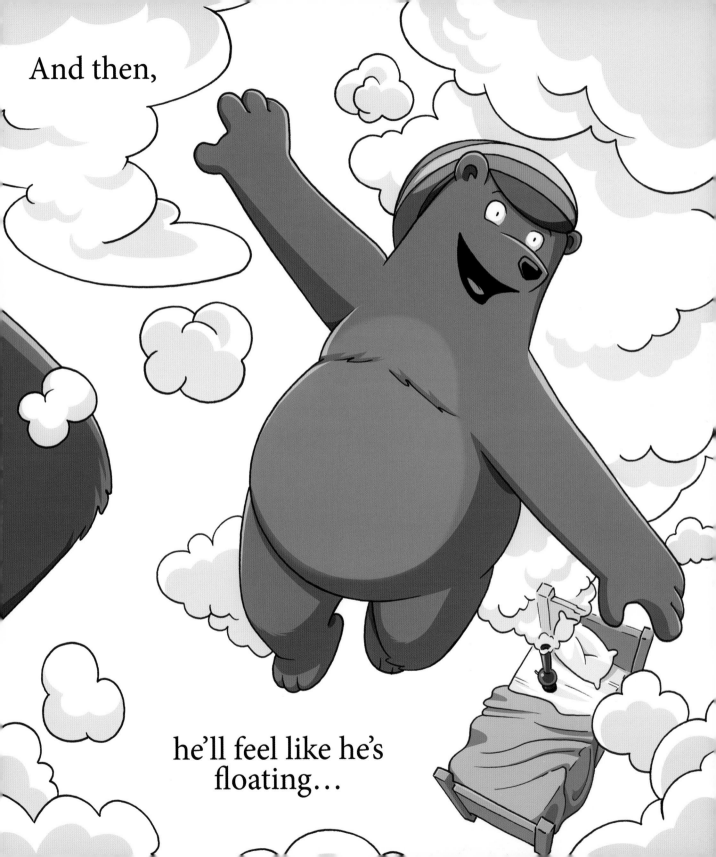

And then,

he'll feel like he's
floating…

But he's not.

The bed will remind him of life.

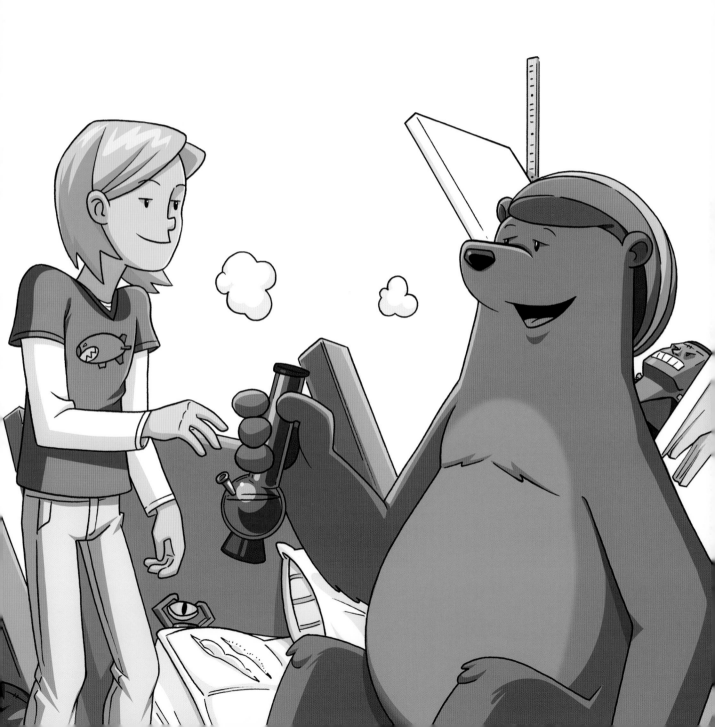

He'll tell you nothing
is forever... Not even beds...
Not even forever.

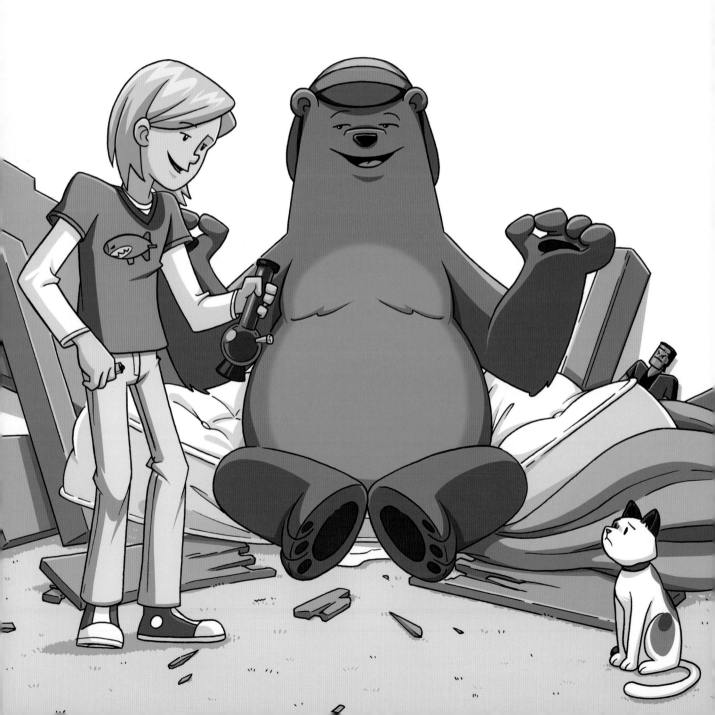

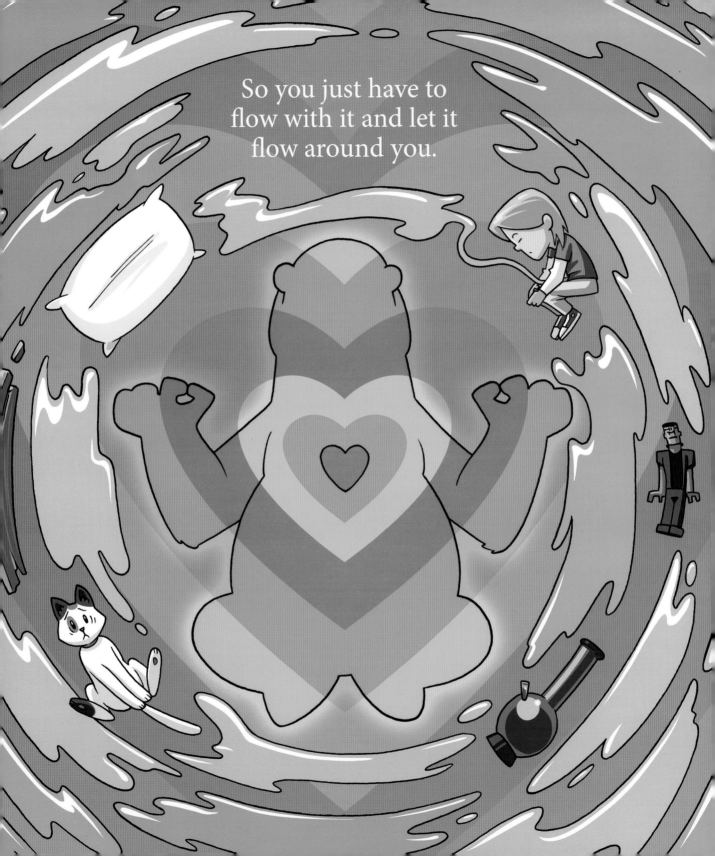

So you just have to
flow with it and let it
flow around you.

He'll tell you now it all makes sense.
Now he understands…

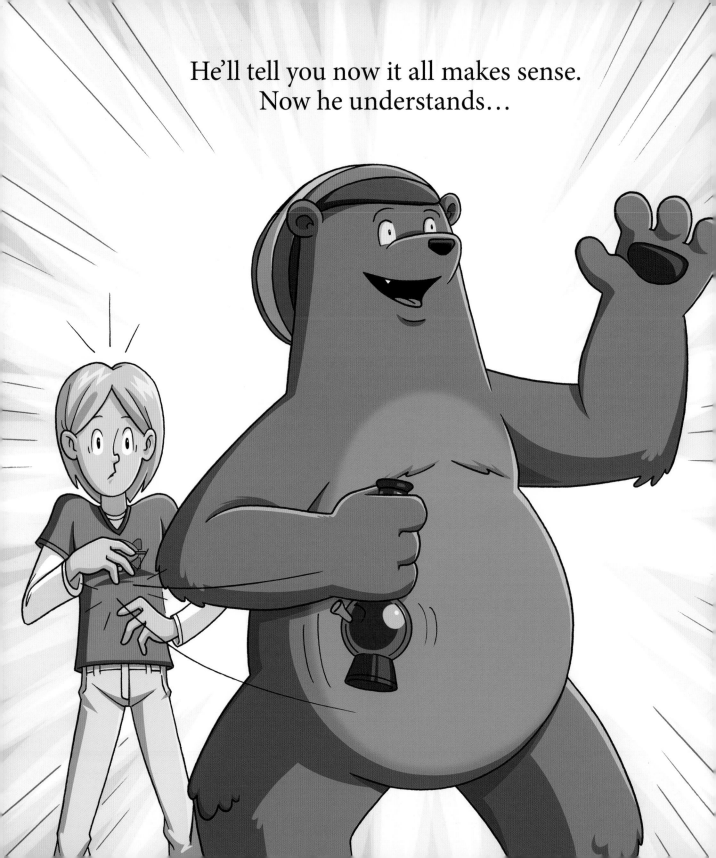

The meaning of life is…

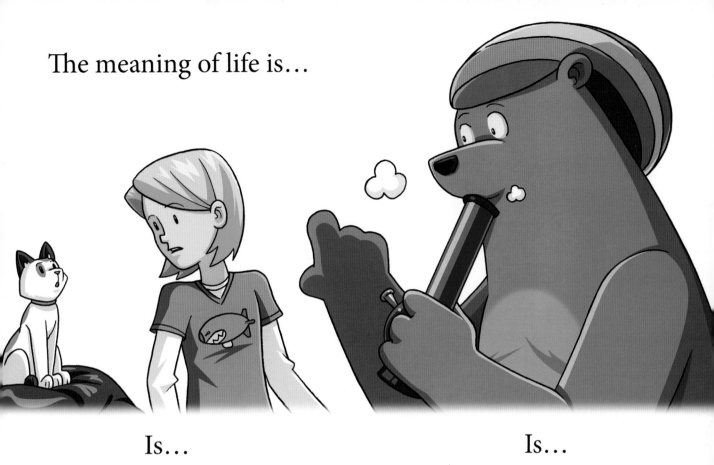

Is…

Is…

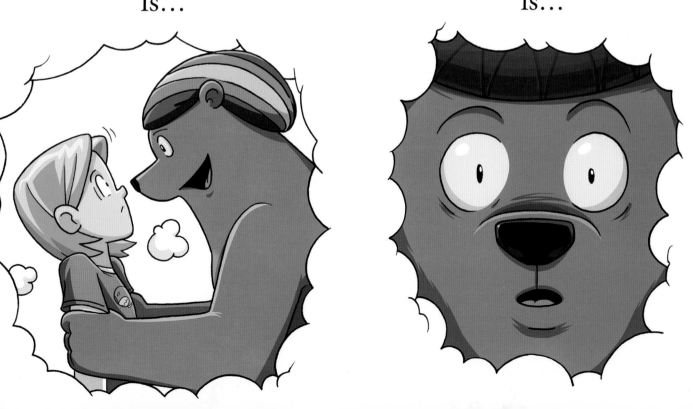

Is that a lava lamp?!?

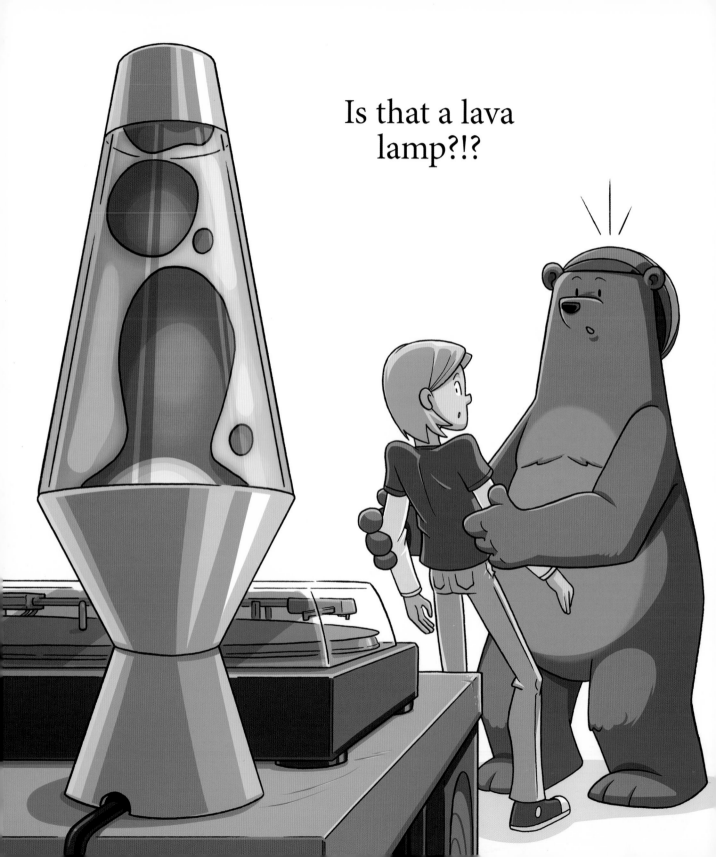

It is! But it's not just any lava lamp.
It's the most amazing lava lamp ever!

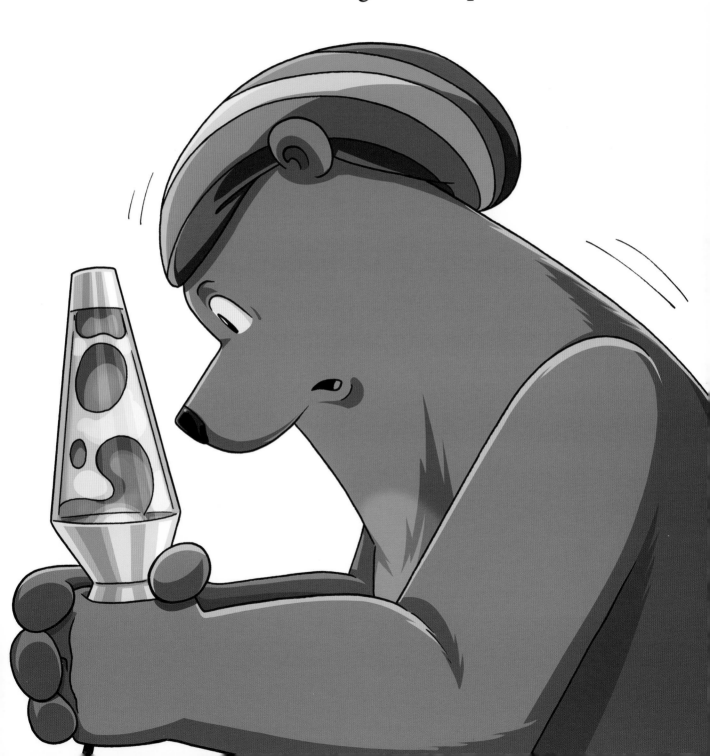

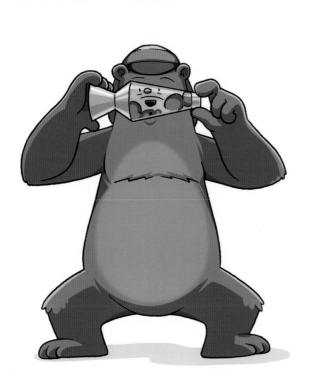

So he'll stare…

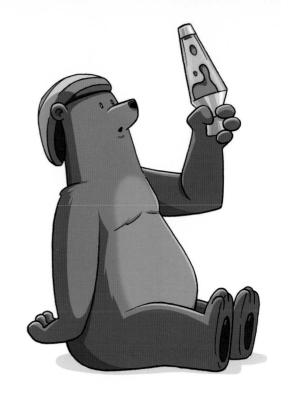

And stare…

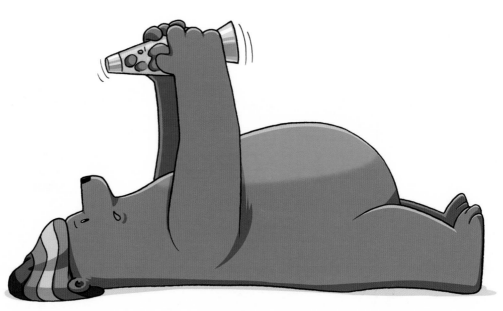

And stare.

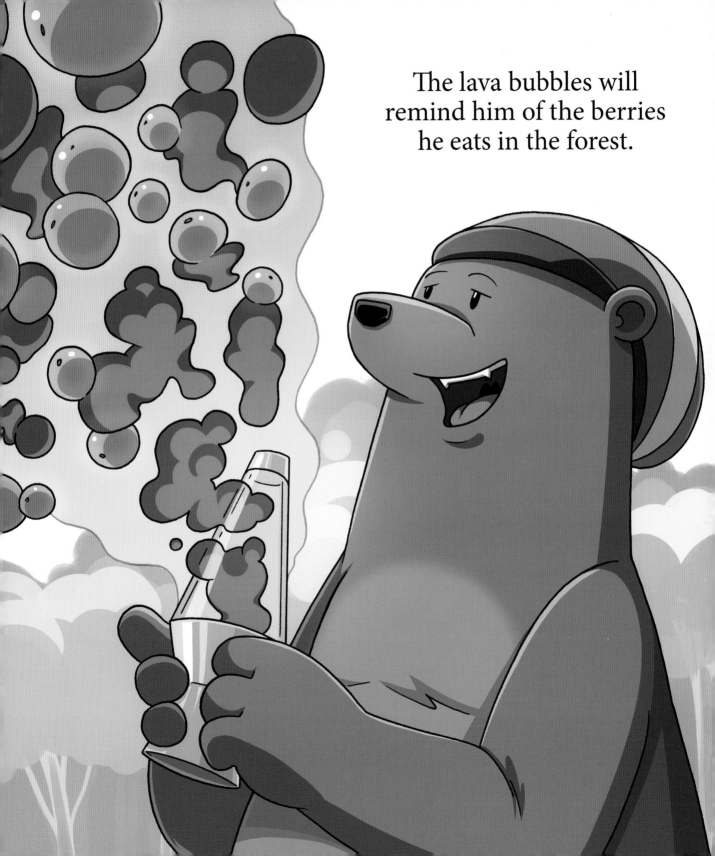

The lava bubbles will remind him of the berries he eats in the forest.

Thinking about the
berries will make him very,
very, hungry.

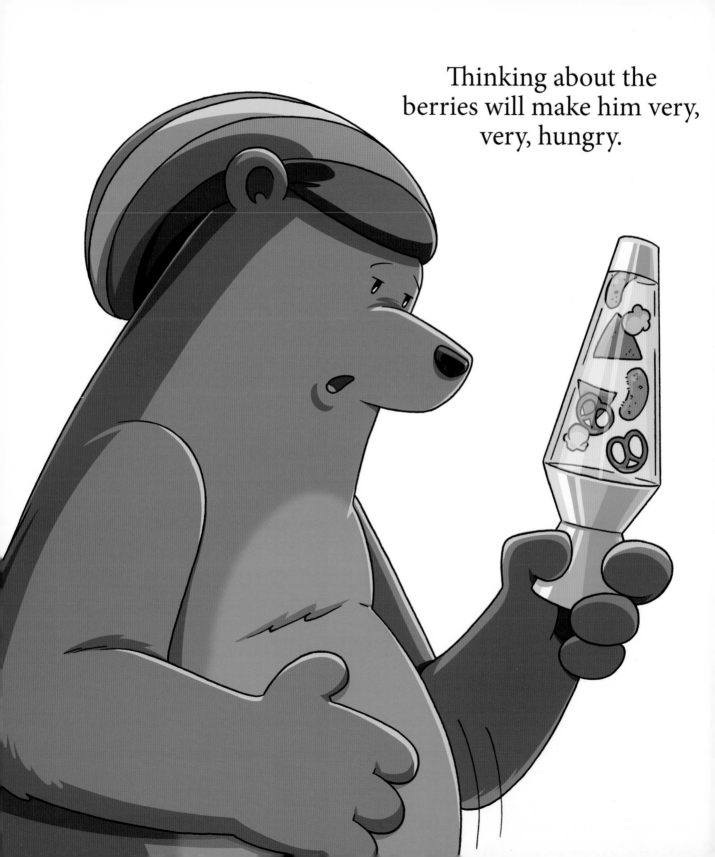

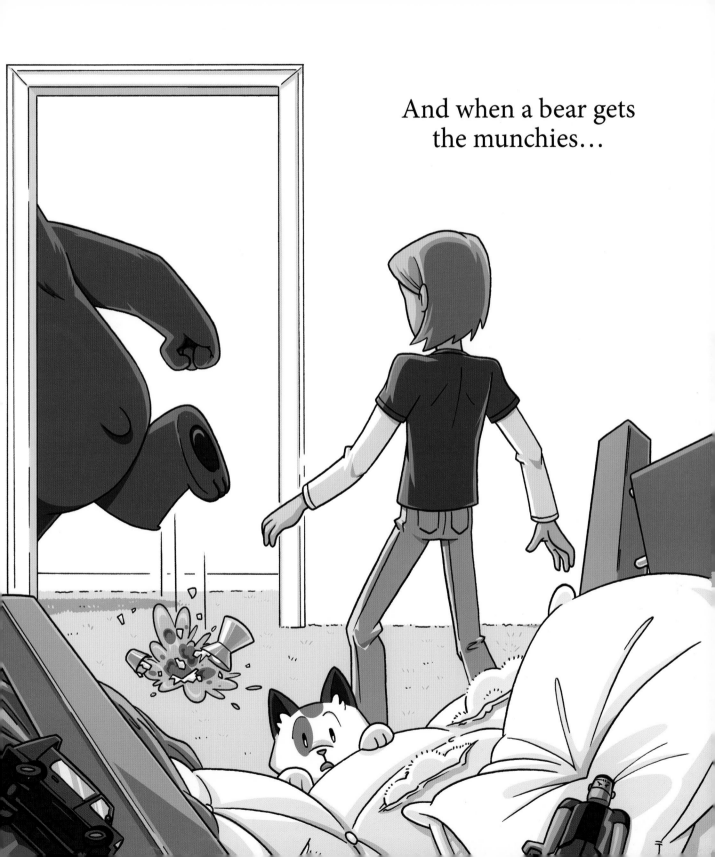

And when a bear gets the munchies…

He gets the MUNCHIES!!!

CAT
SODA

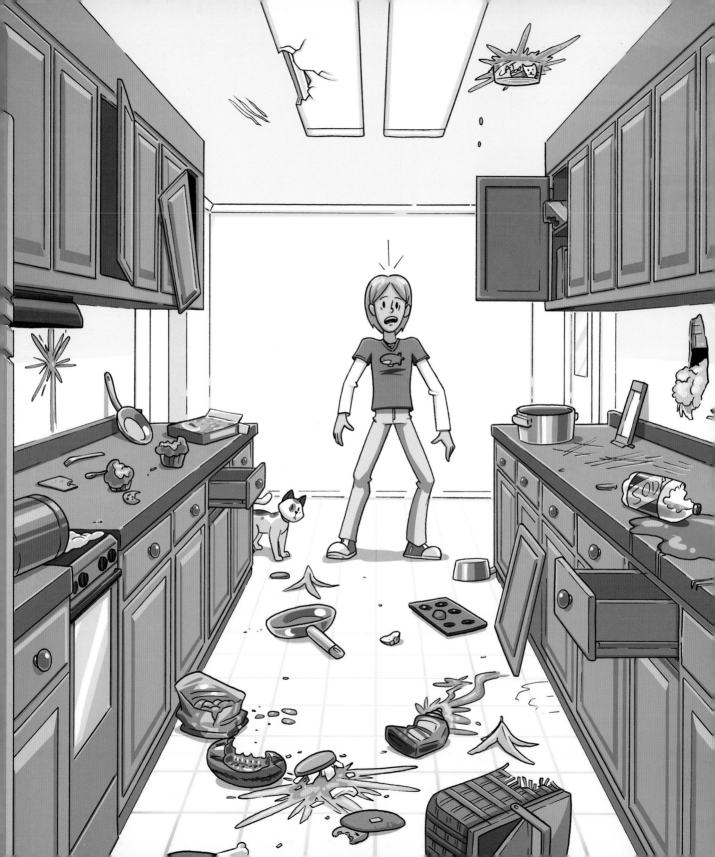

BIG
MAYO

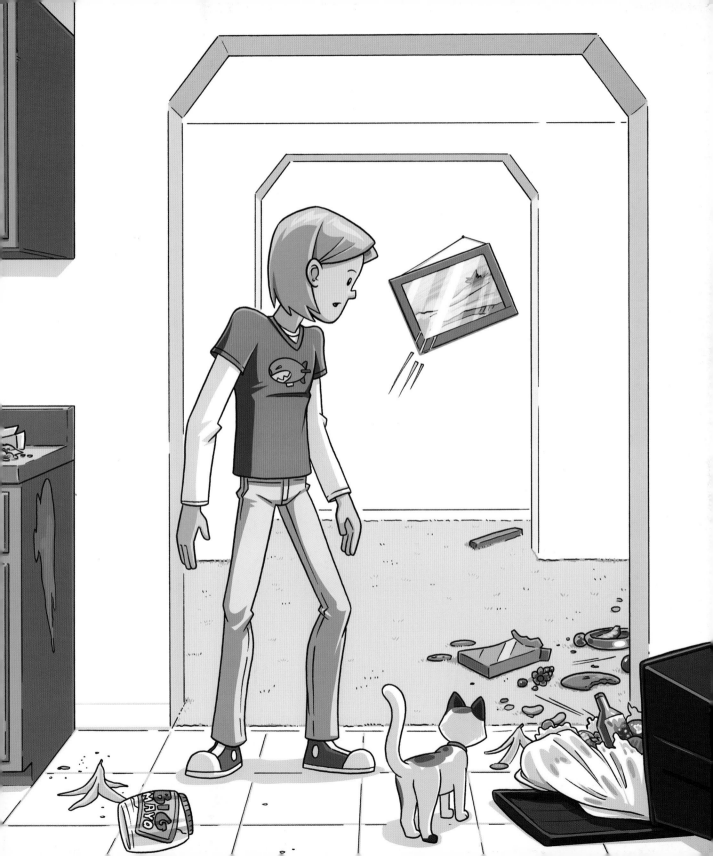

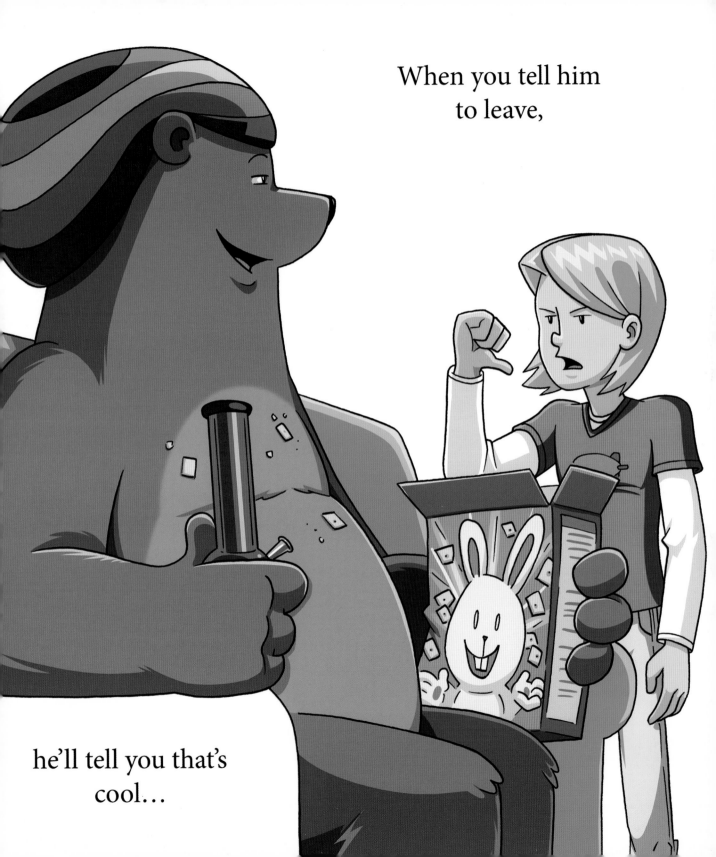

When you tell him
to leave,

he'll tell you that's
cool…

But he can't because he's
couch-locked.

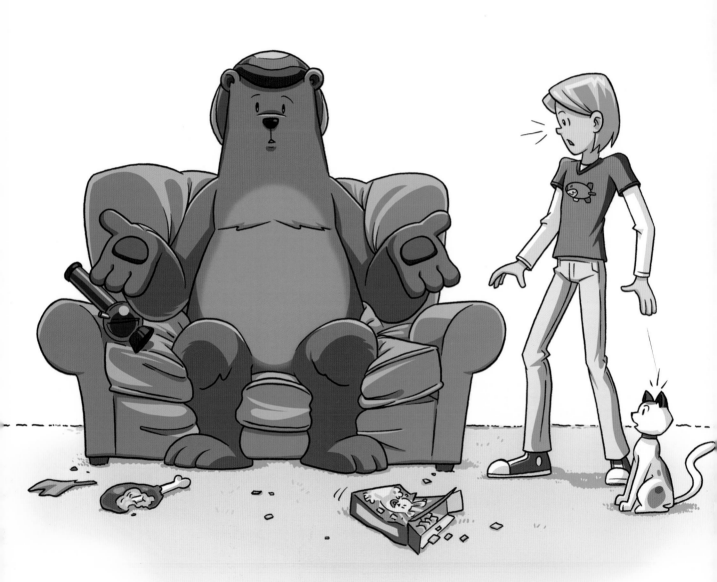

And anyway, the movie he's watching is the funniest one he's ever seen.

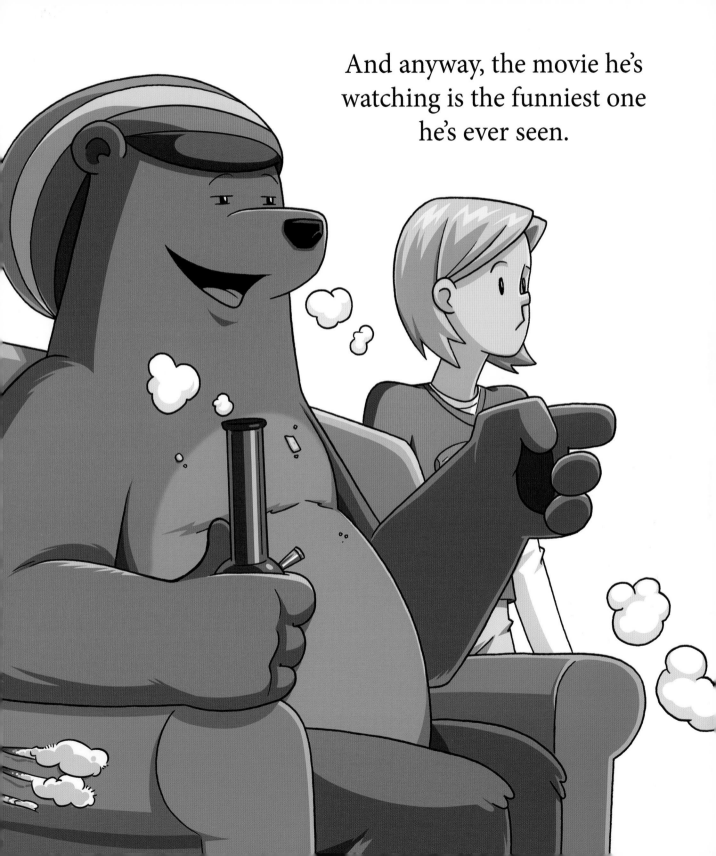

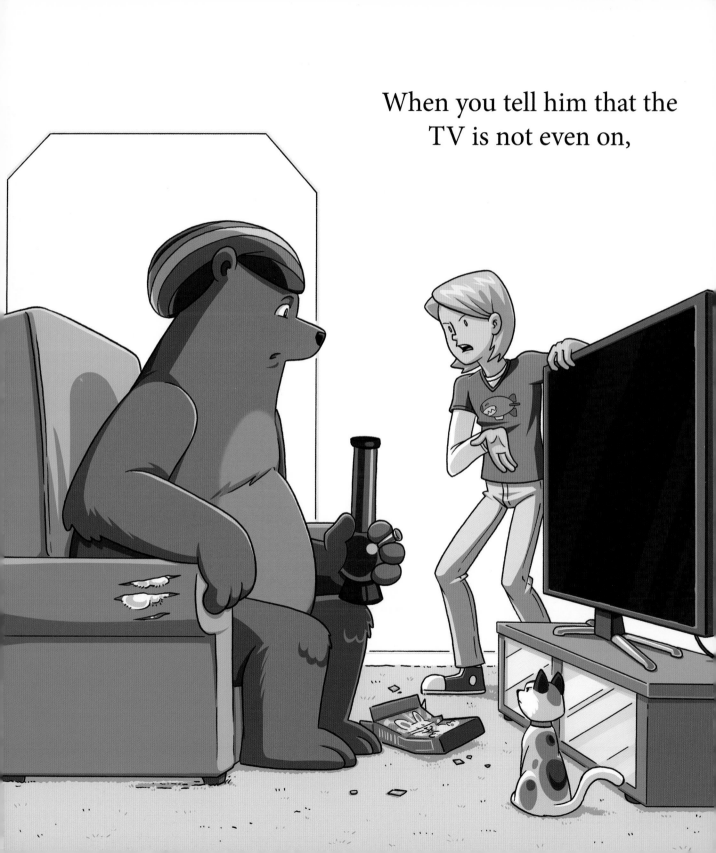

When you tell him that the TV is not even on,

he'll tell you that makes
it even funnier.

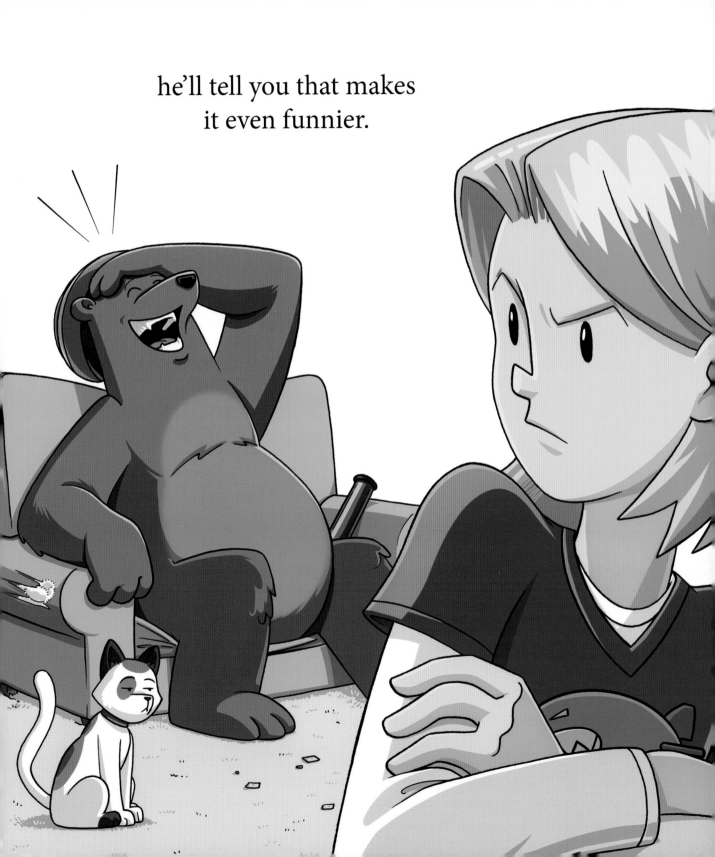

HA HA
HA
HA
HA
HA

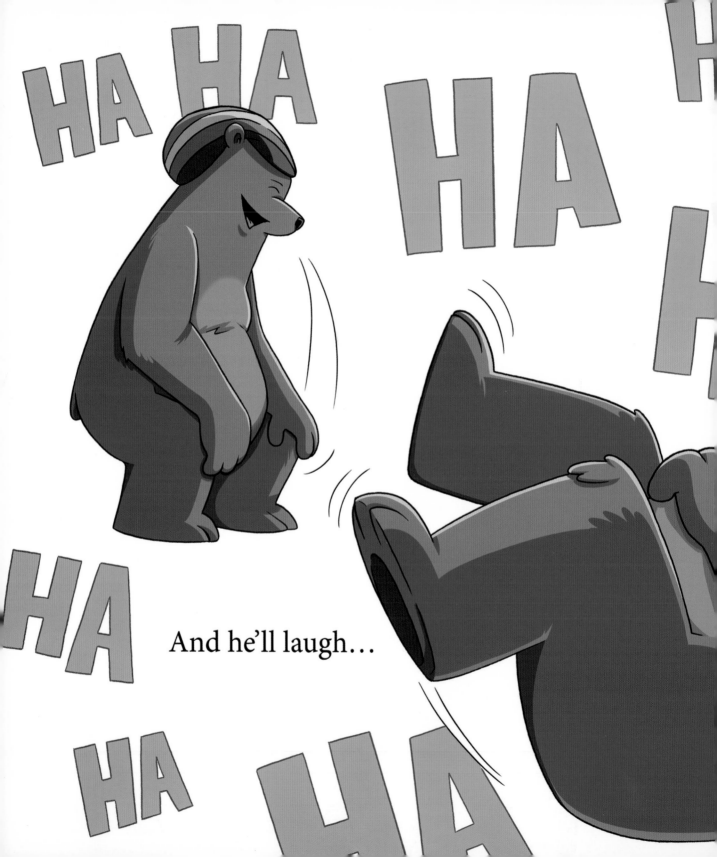

And he'll laugh…

And laugh…

HA
HA
HA
HA
HA
HA

And laugh…

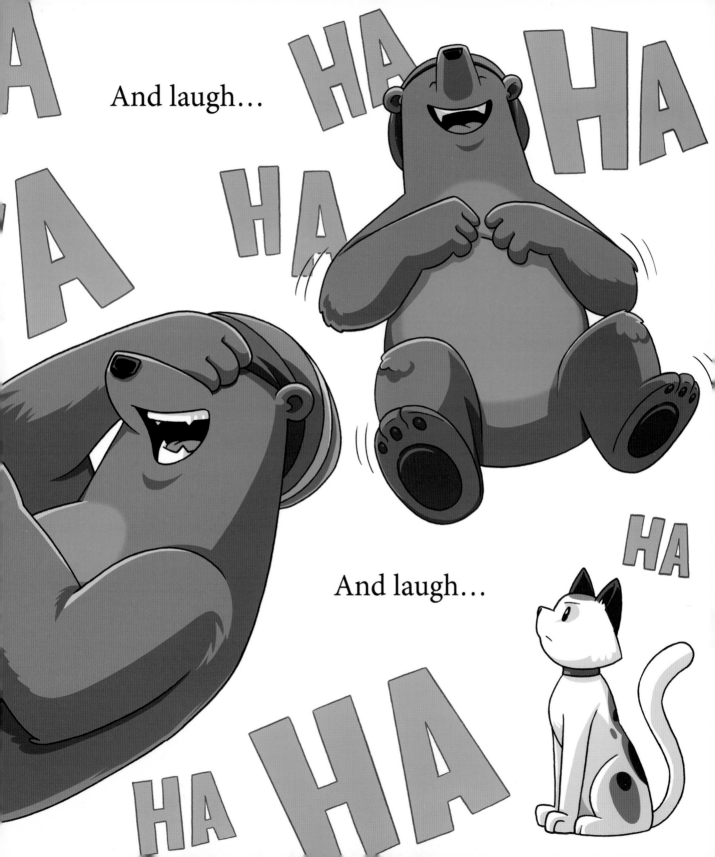

Until...

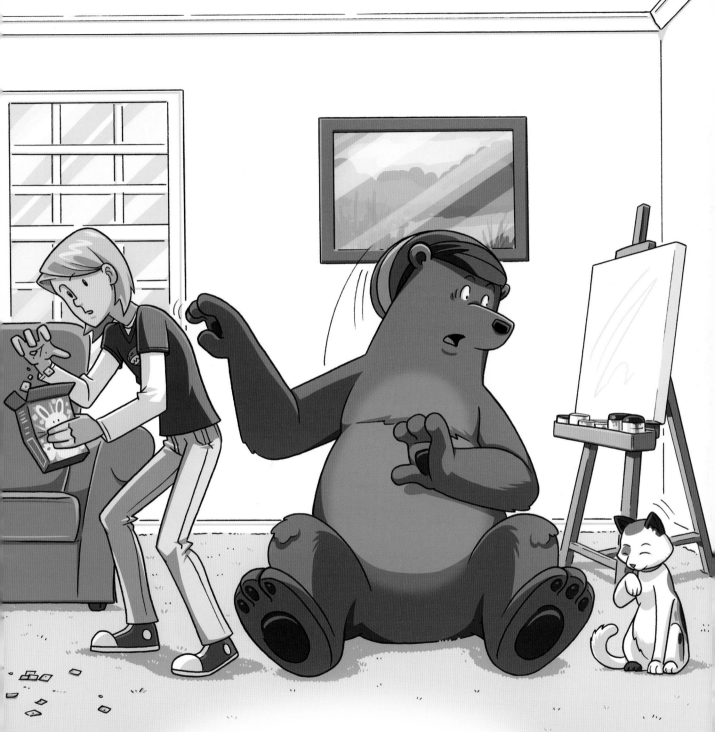

He'll ask you why the cat
is looking at him like that.

Is he laughing
too loud?

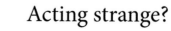

Acting strange?

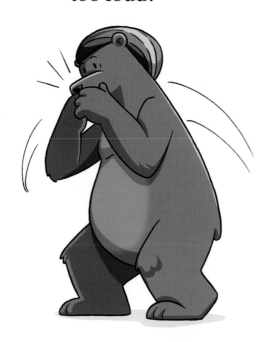

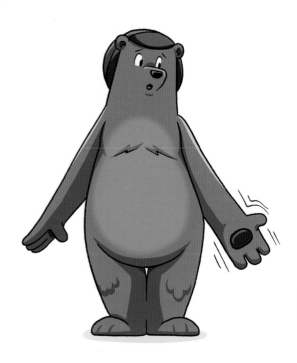

Talking funny?

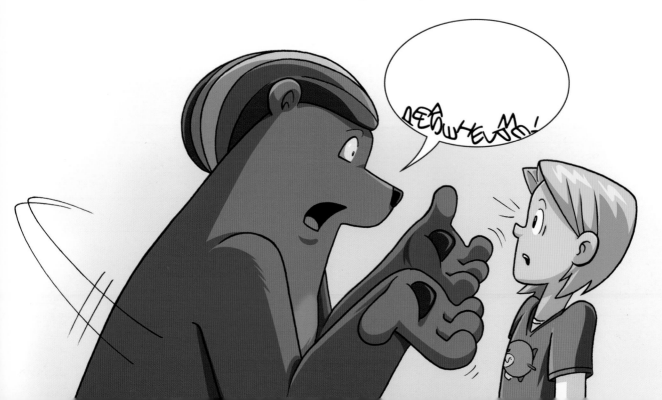

Or maybe…

Just maybe…

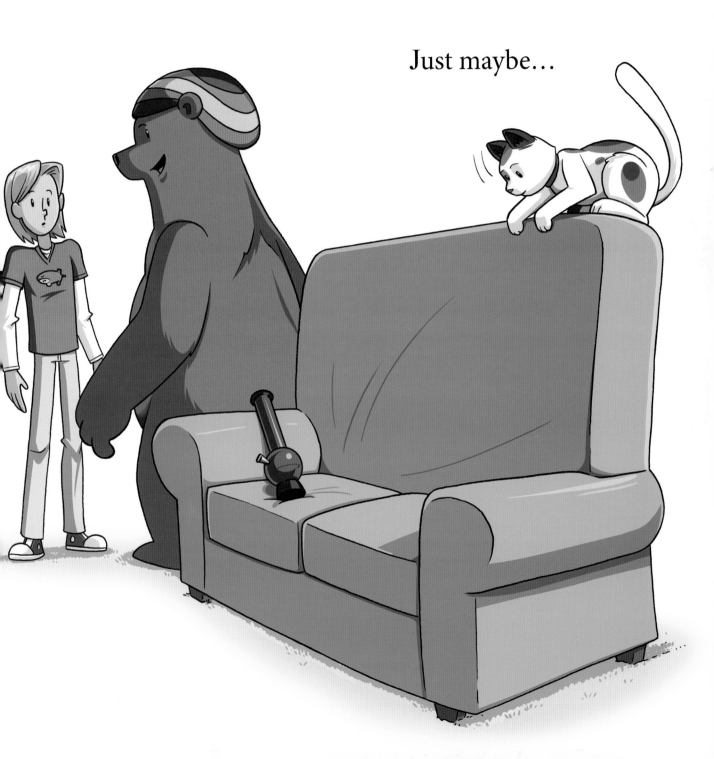

That cat needs to chill.

He'll tell you we'd all get along if we just got high.

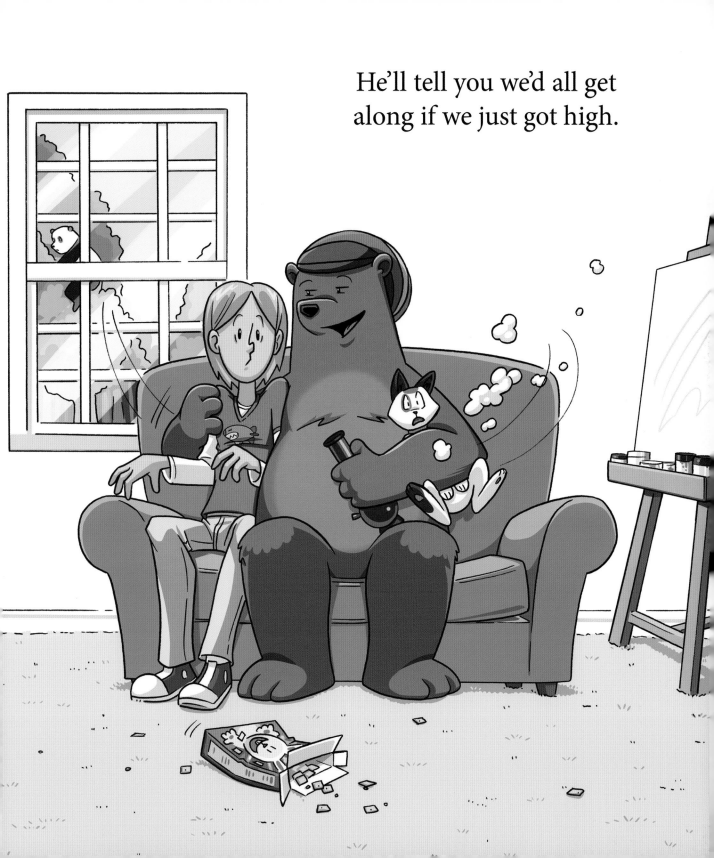

And the world would be
an even better place,

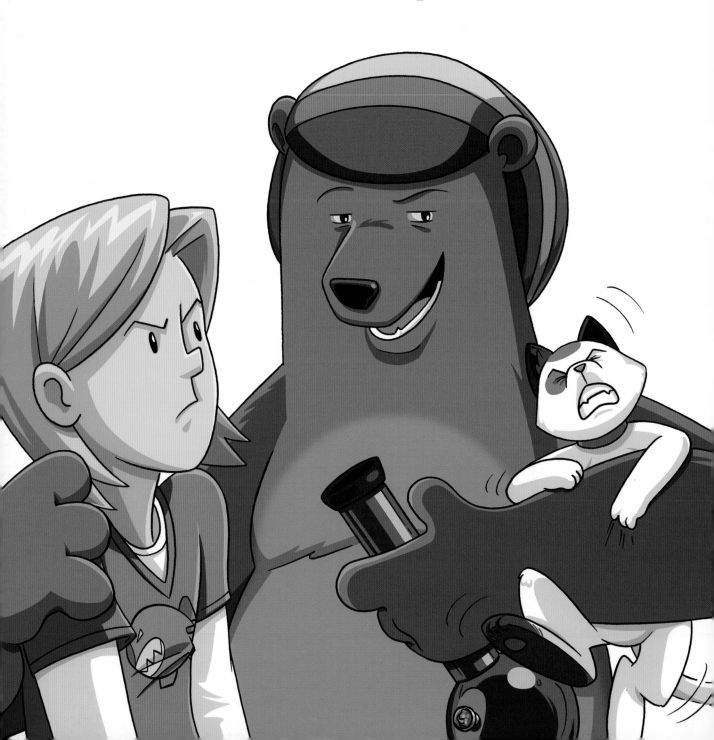

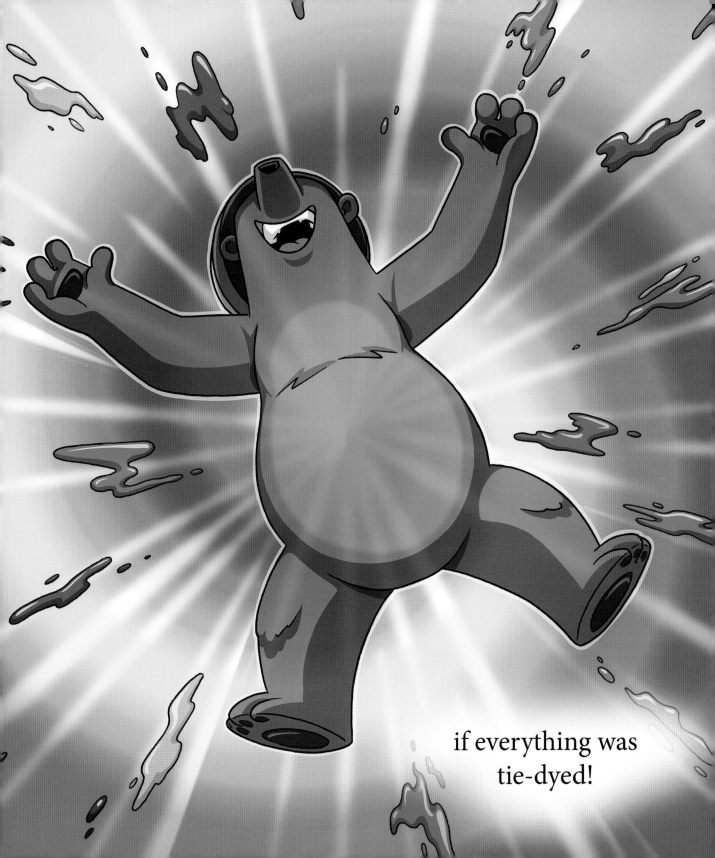

if everything was
tie-dyed!

When you ask him to share,
he says he will...

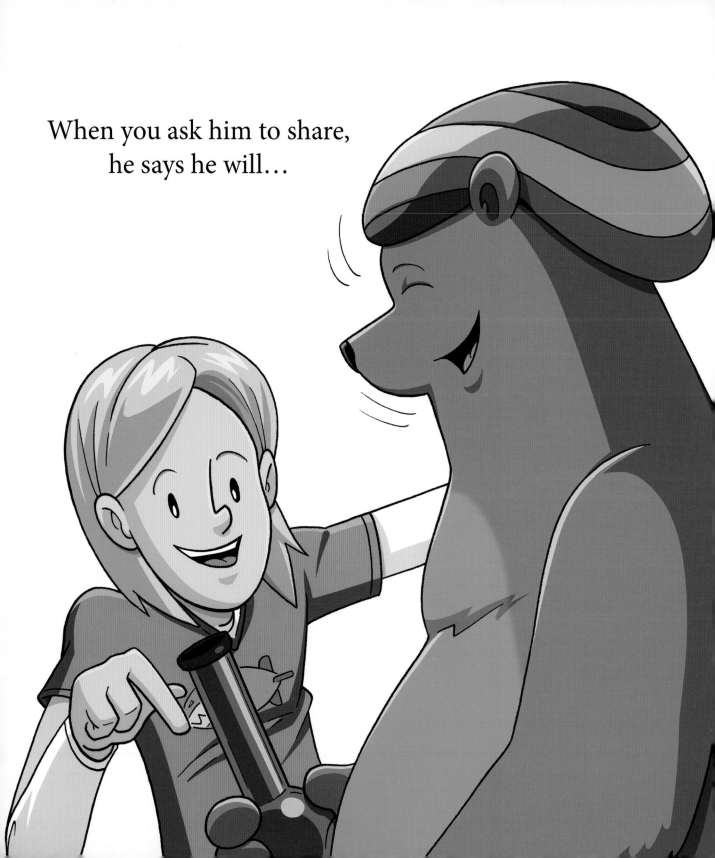

But he'll forget.

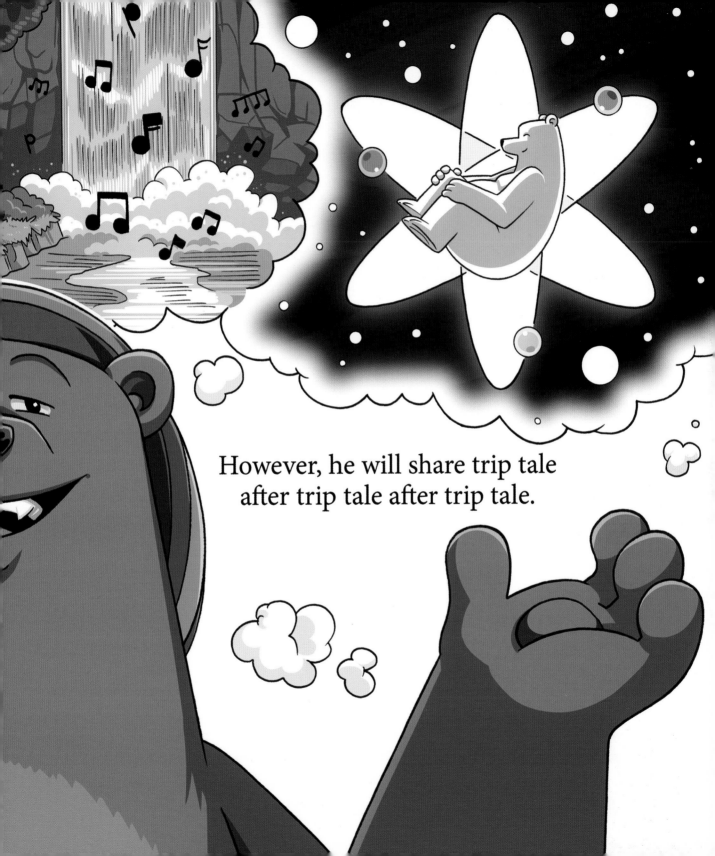

However, he will share trip tale after trip tale after trip tale.

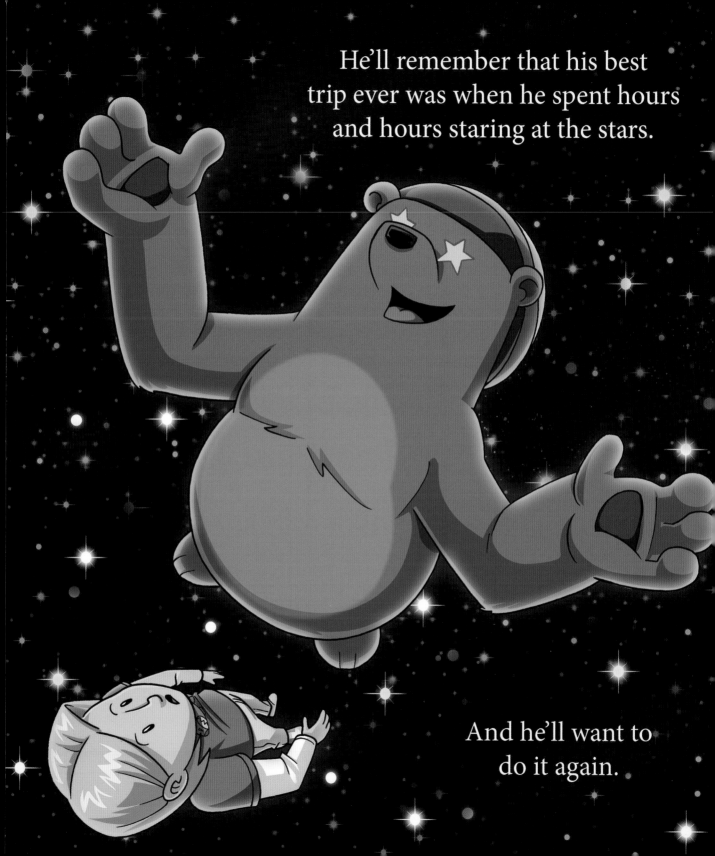

He'll remember that his best trip ever was when he spent hours and hours staring at the stars.

And he'll want to do it again.

But first…

Where did he put
that bong?

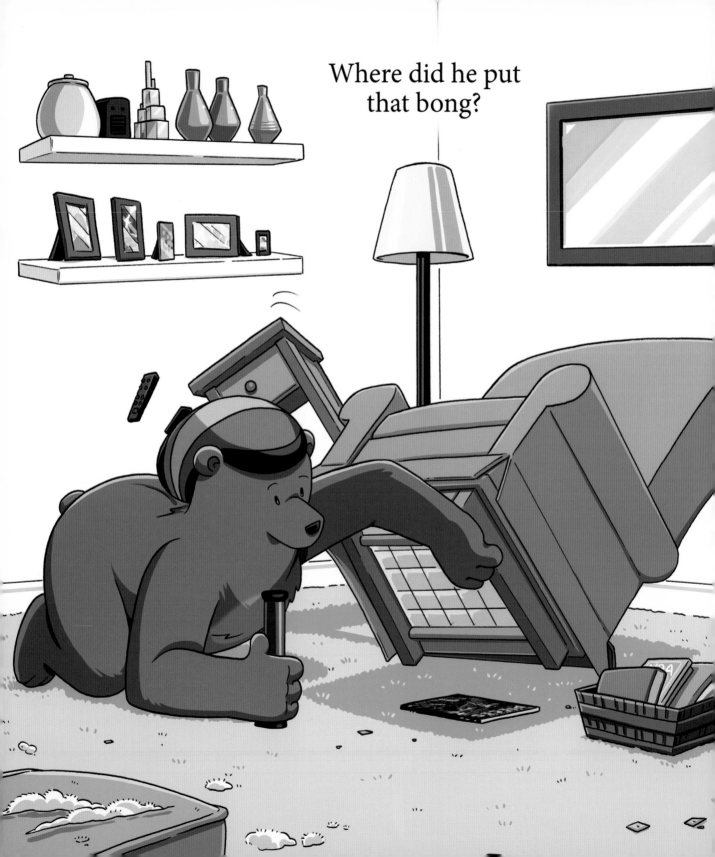

Oh…yeah. Cool.

When he asks if you want
to order pizza, you'll remind him he
was going to look at the stars.

When you wake up
the next morning,
TALBOTT

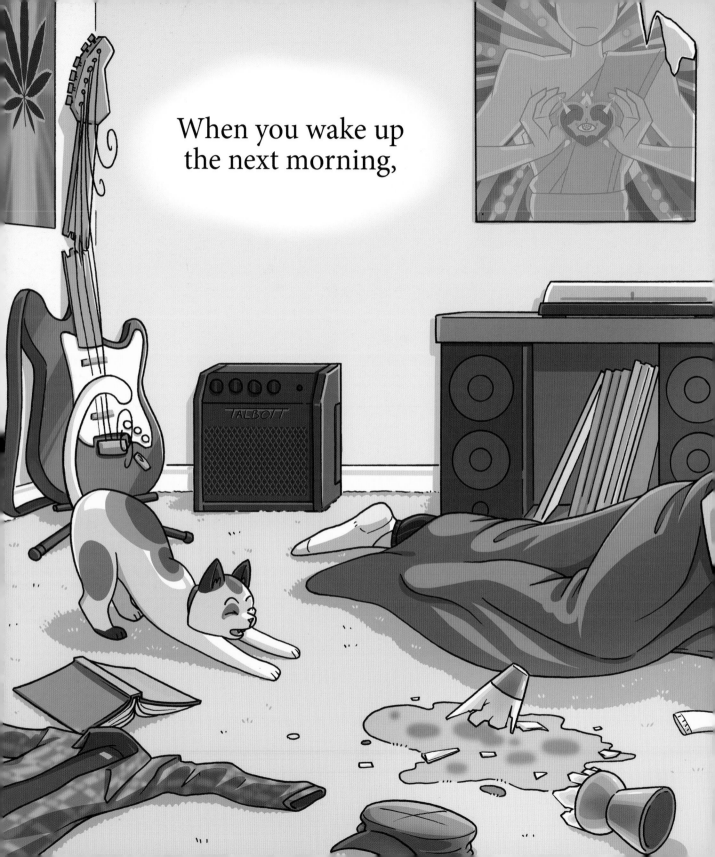

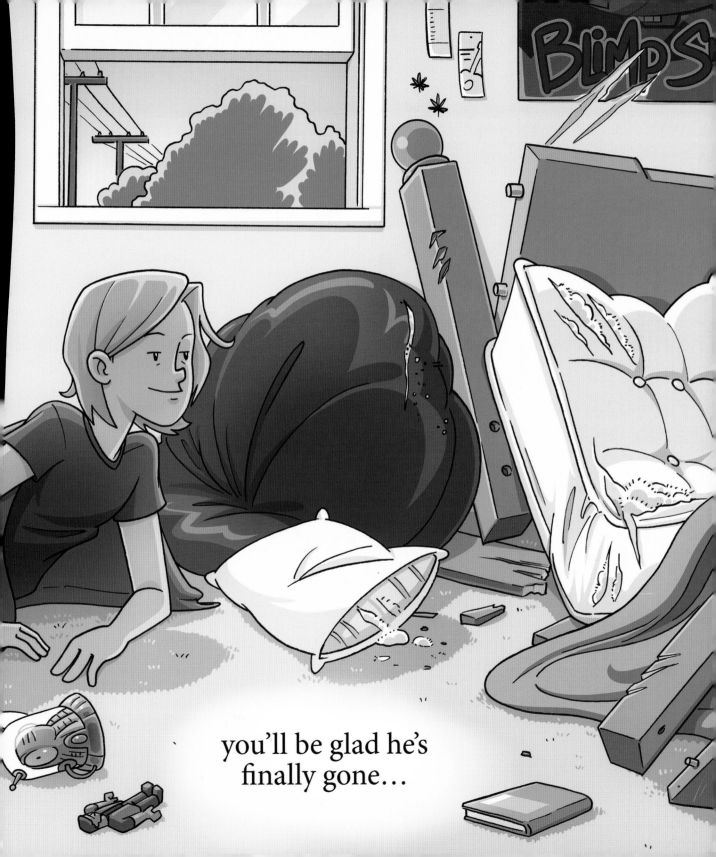

you'll be glad he's
finally gone...

But he's not!

BROWN'S

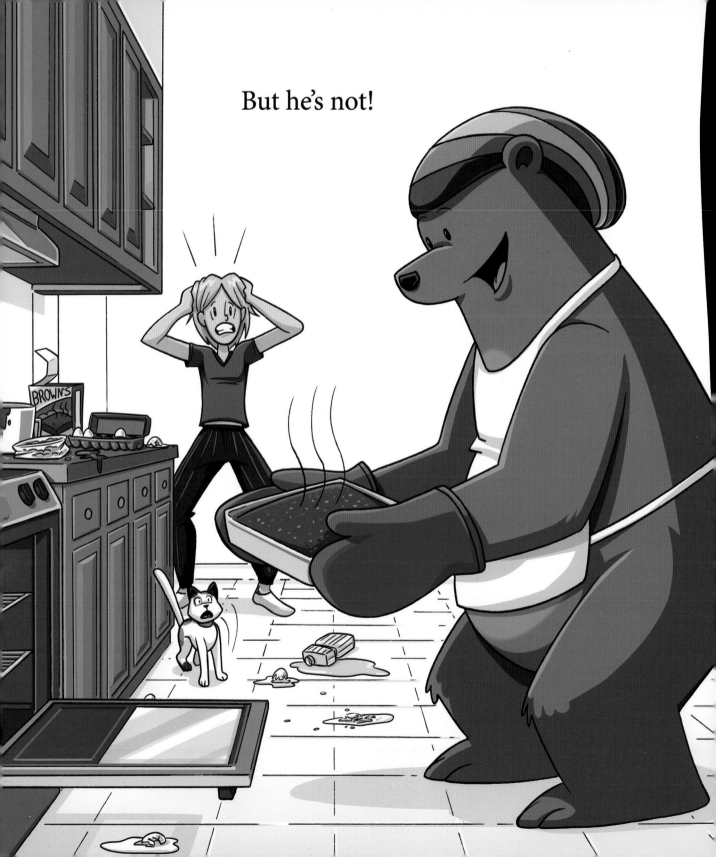

The End

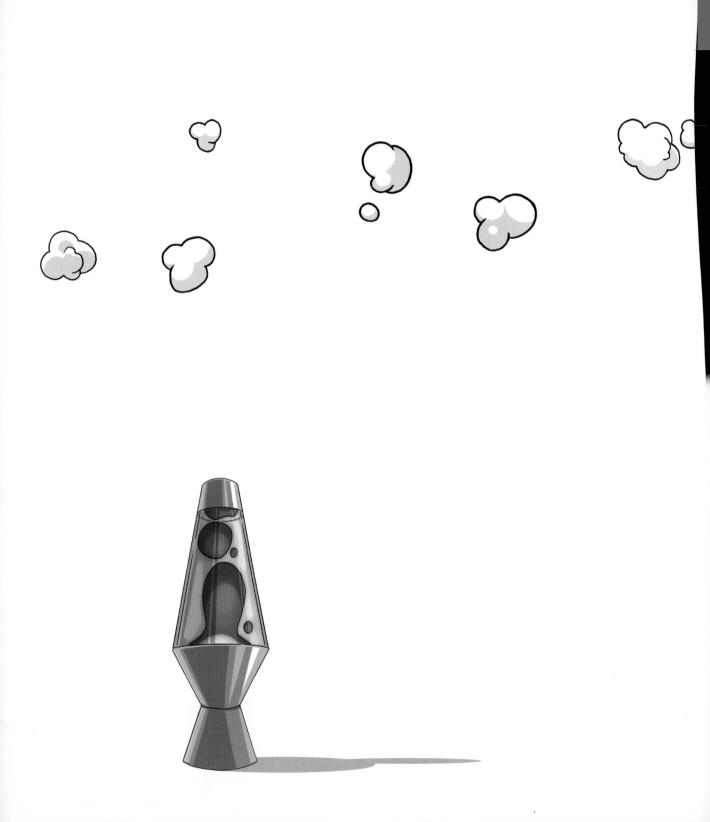

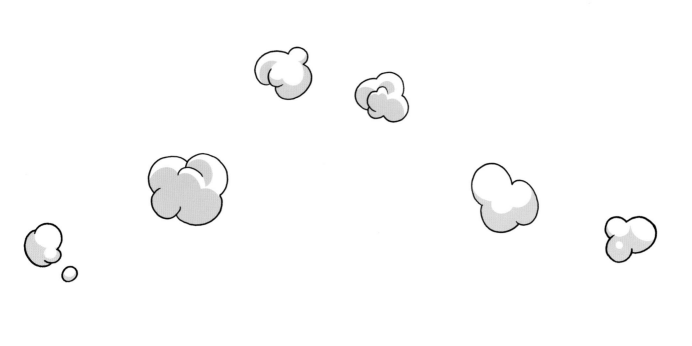